The Wright Brothers

Jason Hook

Illustrated by Peter Lowe

The Bookwright Press
New York · 1989

Great Lives

Beethoven
Louis Braille
Julius Caesar
Captain Cook
Marie Curie
Charles Dickens
Francis Drake
Einstein
Queen Elizabeth I
Queen Elizabeth II
Anne Frank
Gandhi
King Henry VIII
Helen Keller
Joan of Arc

John F. Kennedy
Martin Luther King, Jr.
John Lennon
Ferdinand Magellan
Karl Marx
Mary Queen of Scots
Mozart
Napoleon
Florence Nightingale
Elvis Presley
Richard the Lionhearted
William Shakespeare
Tchaikovsky
Mother Teresa
The Wright Brothers

First published in the United States in 1989 by
The Bookwright Press
387 Park Avenue South, New York NY 10016

First published in 1989 by
Wayland (Publishers) Limited
61 Western Road, Hove, East Sussex BN3 1JD, England

Library of Congress Cataloging-in-Publication Data
Hook, Jason.
   The Wright Brothers / by Jason Hook ; [illustrated by Peter Lowe].
     p. cm. – (Great lives)
   Bibliography: p.
   Includes index.
   Summary: A biography of the two brothers who built and flew the
first powered airplane in 1903.
   ISBN 0–531–18279–7
   1. Wright, Wilbur, 1867–1912 – Juvenile literature. 2. Wright,
Orville, 1871–1948 – Juvenile literature. 3. Aeronautics–United
States–Biography–Juvenile literature. [1. Wright, Wilbur,
–Biography.] I. Lowe, Peter, ill. II. Title. III. Series: Great
lives (New York, N.Y.)
TL540.W7H66 1989
629.13′092′2–dc19   88–38624
[B]   CIP
[92]   AC

Phototypeset by Kalligraphics Ltd, Horley, Surrey
Printed in Italy by G. Canale C.S.p.A., Turin

Contents

The first flight

On the morning of December 17, 1903, an icy wind whipped up the sands at the Kill Devil Hills, near Kitty Hawk in North Carolina. Orville and Wilbur Wright stood clutching the spruce supports for the muslin and wire wings of their Flyer airplane.
Five men from the nearby life-saving station gathered around, waiting to see if this flying machine really would leave the ground.

Until this date, people had taken to the skies only in gliders and gas-filled balloons. Powered airplanes had succeeded only in hopping along the ground, and true flight remained an unfulfilled dream.

Orville lay across the lower wing, in the pilot's cradle, and clasped the controls. The engine spluttered into life, driving two bicycle chains which rotated the Flyer's pusher propellers. A holding rope was eased loose, and the aircraft rolled forward, its wooden supports resting on a low

The brothers telegraphed news of the world's first successful flight to their father.

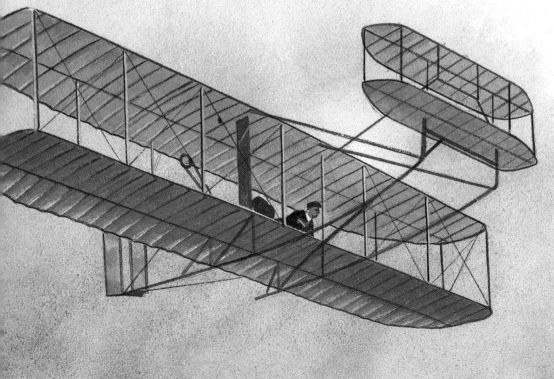

trolley which ran along an iron-shod rail. Wilbur ran alongside steadying the wings, leaving deep footprints in the soft sand. The Flyer rose slowly into the air, and the shutter of a glass-plate camera snapped, capturing the historic moment forever. For 12 seconds the Flyer soared unsteadily through the air, rising and falling constantly, before swooping down into the sand some 118ft (36m) from the launching rail.

This first airplane flight was an incredible achievement, heralding the start of a new age. The brothers flew three more times that day, and in the afternoon telegraphed their father: "Success. Four flights Thursday morning all against twenty-one-mile wind started from level with engine power alone. Average speed through air nearly 31 miles. Longest 57 seconds. Inform Press. Home Christmas."

Early days

Wilbur (right) age thirteen and Orville (left) age nine, before moving back to Dayton.

Wilbur's and Orville's father, Milton Wright, became a minister in the United Brethren Church in 1850. He married Susan Koerner, and preached throughout southeastern Indiana, where their sons Reuchlin and Lorin were born. Wilbur was born in 1867 on a farm near Millville, shortly before Milton Wright's appointment as editor of his church newspaper caused the family to move to Dayton, Ohio. Here Orville and his younger sister Katharine were born. Milton Wright's election as a bishop caused further changes

of home, before the Wright family settled permanently in Dayton in 1884.

Milton Wright encouraged his children to investigate anything that aroused their curiosity, and to earn pocket money through their own invention. By the age of nine, Orville was studying the effects of water pressure. He once built a lathe, while Wilbur constructed a machine to fold the church newspaper.

The Wright brothers inherited their mother's ability to "mend anything," and excelled at school in mathematics and engineering. They were very close, and Wilbur later recalled: "From the time we were little children . . . Orville and myself lived together, played together, worked together and, in fact, thought together. We talked over our thoughts and aspirations so that nearly everything that was done in our lives has been the result of conversations, suggestions and discussions between us."

They gained an interest in flight at a very early age, when their father gave them a toy helicopter designed by French aviation pioneer Alphonse Penaud. This model of bamboo, cork and paper could actually fly, powered by a twisted rubber spring. Fascinated, Orville and Wilbur immediately built their own models and watched with delight as they spun up into the air.

The young brothers launching a toy Penaud helicopter.

Newspapers and bicycles

The first public success of the brothers' lifelong partnership came in March, 1889, when they began writing, editing and publishing a weekly newspaper, the *West Side News*.

From the age of twelve, Orville had shown a special interest in printing. From experiments with engraved wood blocks smeared with ink, he progressed to printing the school newspaper, *The Midget*, using a press obtained by Wilbur and type purchased by their father. Meanwhile, Wilbur was recovering from a serious injury suffered while playing ice hockey. Wilbur also spent much of his time nursing his mother, before her death on July 4, 1889.

Orville spent two summers working for a Dayton printer before Wilbur helped him build a printing press large enough to produce the *West Side News*. It .was a great success, and the following year Orville published a daily newspaper called the *Evening Item*, edited by Wilbur. After four months, though, competition from the four established Dayton dailies forced them out of business. The brothers tried again, printing the weekly, *Snapshots*, but their interest was slowly turning to a business more suited to their mechanical expertise.

The "safety" bicycle had recently become very popular: with two wheels of equal size and fitted with air-filled tires, it was replacing the old-fashioned penny-farthings. The brothers each bought a bicycle, and shortly afterward opened a shop selling the machines and their accessories. They added a repair shop, then moved to larger premises and started manufacturing their own models. The brothers first built and sold the Van Cleve bicycle, named after a Dutch ancestor, and then produced their most popular $18 Wright Special. They had learned the importance of publicity from their early experiences in the newspaper business, and through clever advertising, Wilbur and Orville were soon able to build the Wright Cycle Company into a thriving business.

Orville and Wilbur printing their weekly four-page newspaper, the West Side News.

A new interest

The spark which ignited the Wright brothers' interest in flight came with the death of German aviation pioneer Otto Lilienthal in 1896. While Wilbur and Orville had been building bicycles, Lilienthal had made over 2,000 hang-gliding flights in the Rhinower Hills, near Berlin. They had seen magazine photographs of Lilienthal soaring high on beautiful bird-like wings, and reports of his fatal crash focused the brothers' interest on aviation.

They read what books they could find, including Professor

Otto Lilienthal's gliding flights inspired the brothers.

Marey's *Animal Mechanism* and other studies of bird flight. In 1899, Wilbur wrote to the Smithsonian Institution in Washington D.C., requesting more publications, and declaring his belief, "that simple flight at least is possible to man."

The brothers hungrily devoured all the information sent to them. They were particularly influenced by the American pioneer Octave Chanute's *Progress in Flying Machines*, which recorded the achievements of aviation pioneers before 1894. All of these men had attempted to maintain balance in flight by shifting the weight of the pilot's body. Wilbur, though, saw that buzzards maintained their stability by twisting their wing-tips. He concluded that if an airplane's wings could be twisted in the same manner, altering each wing's resistance to

Orville and Wilbur start work on their first glider.

gusts of wind, the airplane could also be balanced.

That August, the brothers constructed a biplane kite, its 5ft (1.5m) wings braced so that they could be warped according to Wilbur's theory, by two control lines. Wilbur set out alone to fly the kite, and found it could be controlled successfully. Equipped with this knowledge, and with their bicycle premises providing a perfect workshop, the Wright brothers prepared to build their first flying machine.

Leaving the ground

While the brothers' first flying machine took shape in the back of their Dayton bicycle shop, Wilbur sent letters to the United States weather bureau and Octave Chanute, seeking advice on where they might find winds strong enough to lift it. Following their recommendations Wilbur contacted the weather station at Kitty Hawk on the North Carolina coast, where he headed after the glider's completion in September, 1900.

Following Orville's arrival shortly afterward, the brothers camped on the desolate Kitty Hawk sand dunes and assembled their first glider. It was based upon their original kite, with biplane wings of 17ft (5.18m) span, a front elevator to control its vertical movement, but no tail. They flew it first as an enormous kite, each brother controlling a wing by means of two wires. Then they each made gliding flights, lying on the bottom wing and soaring up into

The Wrights tested their glider by flying it as a kite.

12

the air for the first time. Their flying machine was a success, and they returned excitedly to Dayton, Wilbur enthusing: "When once a machine is under proper control under all conditions, the motor problem will be quickly solved."

After another busy season in their workshop, the brothers emerged the following summer with their new, second glider, boasting a much larger wingspan. They transported it to the Kill Devil Hills, just south of Kitty Hawk, where they were joined by the enthusiastic Chanute.

The brothers became disillusioned after testing their second glider in bad weather.

Octave Chanute's 1896 glider.

The glider had been designed according to Lilienthal's calculations, but only flew successfully after some major adjustments. The camp was plagued by bad weather and swarms of mosquitoes, and the Wrights departed in August, feeling despondent. Wilbur confided to his younger brother that he didn't think man would fly in a thousand years.

Learning to fly

"Having set out with absolute faith in the existing scientific data, we were driven to doubt one thing after another, till finally, after two years of experiment, we cast it all aside, and decided to rely entirely upon our own investigations."

With this determination, the Wright brothers dedicated a year to conducting extensive research in their workshop. To discover the most effective shape and angle for an airplane's wing, they mounted different surfaces on an upturned wheel, which was rotated by pedaling a bicycle. Next, these self-taught engineers built a magnificent wind-tunnel, through which air was driven at about 30mph (50kph) by a large fan. Miniature wings were suspended on delicate balances at the far end of the wind-tunnel, while the Wrights peered

From 1901 on the brothers studied flight in their Dayton workshop.

14

The Wrights regularly flew their third glider with great success.

through a window and noted on scraps of wallpaper how each shape behaved. They tested over a hundred wings, and Orville later remarked that, by 1902, his brother and he knew more about curved surfaces, "a hundred times over, than all our predecessors put together."

In August, the Wrights assembled their third glider, which had an even larger wingspan and rigid tail, at Kill Devil Hills. When the glider crashed on an early test-flight, Orville conceived the idea of making the tail flexible, and connecting it to the controls that warped the wings, creating a rudder. The pilot controlled the front elevator with a control stick, while a harness around his hips enabled him to work wings and rudder together.

The adjustment was a great success, and between September and October, 1902, the Wright brothers made nearly 1,000 flights, the longest lasting 26 seconds and covering almost 650ft (200m). Soaring regularly and breathlessly over the Kill Devil sand dunes, Wilbur and Orville learned to fly.

The Flyer

Returning to Dayton, the Wrights set about adding power to their successful glider. Finding all car engines too heavy, they built their own 12 horse-power motor, weighing under 140lb (63kg). They added the final piece to the jigsaw after months of painstaking research, by building a remarkably efficient propeller, based entirely on their own calculations. On September 25, 1903, the Wrights arrived at Kill Devil with their completed Flyer biplane.

Below: *Taking off on the first successful powered flight.*

Above: *An impression of the flight of December 17, 1903.*

With the brothers on the verge of powered flight, aviation elsewhere had made little progress. In France, only Chanute's lecture on the Wright gliders in April had aroused much interest. In the United States, Samuel Langley's much-publicized Aerodrome machine had been launched recently from a floating catapult; and nose-dived straight into the Potomac River.

After set-backs due to mechanical problems and bad weather, the Wrights, on December 14, hoisted a flag over their camp to inform friends at the life-saving station of the Flyer's maiden flight. After winning the toss of a coin, Wilbur guided the machine skyward.

He hauled too hard on the elevator though; the Flyer stalled, crashing into the sand.

After repairs, Orville, three days later, made his historic flight, which he described as, "the first in the history of the world in which a machine carrying a man had raised itself by its own power into the air in full flight, had sailed forward without reduction of speed and had finally landed at a point as high as that from which it started."

The brothers made three more flights that day, with Wilbur achieving 852ft (259m) in 57 seconds. The Flyer never left the ground again, but its success, according to a historian, marked "the beginning of a new era in the history of the world."

Spreading their wings

"The age of flight has come at last," Wilbur declared upon returning to Dayton. Yet few newspapers carried the story of the first flight. Those that did printed exaggerated reports, which caused the public to scoff at the Wrights' claims.

Leaving mechanic Charlie Taylor to mind the bicycle business, Orville and Wilbur quietly continued their work, designing an excellent new airplane and engine. In May 1904, they tested the Flyer II at Huffman Prairie, a large cow pasture near Dayton, lent to

them provided all cattle were herded away from the airplane's flight-path! When poor weather and mechanical failures disrupted Flyer II's early take-off attempts, watching reporters added to their claims that the Wrights were frauds.

As the year progressed, though, the airplane flew with increasing regularity. A pulley operated by dropping a weight from a tall pylon was successfully introduced in September to assist in take-off. Later that month, Wilbur made the first ever circular flight. It was witnessed by a local man named Amos Root, who published an eye-witness account in his magazine, *Gleanings in Bee Culture.*

The following year, the Wrights constructed their Flyer III, the world's first fully practical airplane. From June to October 1905, they flew regularly from Huffman Prairie. Only the Flyer III's fuel supply limited their achievements, and Wilbur made one flight of 24.5mi (39km), lasting 38 minutes and 3 seconds.

The brothers, however, were still waiting for a patent to be

Flying above the Ohio farmers.

granted, preventing anyone from copying their invention. So, they refused to allow anyone other than themselves to photograph Flyer III. Consequently, while Ohio farmers grew used to Wilbur and Orville soaring overhead in their magnificent machine, the world continued to insist that it was impossible for humans to fly.

Wilbur tests the wind before a flight at Huffman Prairie, the world's first aerodrome.

Flyers or liars?

From October 16, 1905 to May 6, 1908 the Wright brothers locked away their airplanes and gave up flying. They were exasperated by the public's refusal to accept their claims, and by their failure to obtain a buyer for their invention.

In January 1905, the brothers had written to the American and British governments, offering the sale of their Flyer III airplane for military purposes. Negotiations with the British plodded on inconclusively, while the U.S. War Department refused to believe that the airplane even existed! The Wrights offered twice more to demonstrate their claims, but were rudely rebuffed by the American government.

After a year of negotiations with the French, the Wrights traveled to Paris in the summer

Wilbur (left) and Orville, photographed in 1910.

Newspapers in France continued to question the Wrights' claims.

of 1907 and a modified Flyer, the Type A, was shipped to Le Havre. It remained there when the brothers returned to the United States, having established links with French businessmen and witnessing the inadequacies of European aviation.

The Wrights at last won contracts with the U.S. War Department in February, 1908, and a French syndicate in March, both dependent on demonstration flights. Returning to Kill Devil, they refreshed their piloting skills in the 1905 Flyer III. Seats were added to it, and Wilbur made the world's first passenger flight, taking up mechanic C. W. Furnas.

In May, Wilbur sailed for France to answer once and for all questions raised in the *Paris Herald*, February 10, 1907: "The Wrights have flown or they have not flown. They possess a machine or they do not possess one. They are in fact either flyers or liars . . . It is difficult to fly; it is easy to say 'we have flown'."

Wilbur conquers Europe

Wilbur traveled to a car factory at Le Mans, and uncrated the Type A aircraft which had been in storage since the previous summer. The airplane was severely damaged and Wilbur worked furiously for two months on repairs, while French doubts over his ability to fly grew.

At last, on August 8, 1908, a critical audience of Europe's most famous aviators joined a large crowd at Hunaudières racetrack, near Le Mans. In the afternoon, Wilbur took off in his airplane, flew two graceful circles, and gently landed. The cheering crowd were stunned, casting their hats into the air to salute him; at last the Wrights were heroes.

"Well, we are beaten!" the French pioneer Léon Delagrange exclaimed, "We just don't exist!" European aviation was

Wilbur's flights in France astonished European aviators.

Wilbur at Camp d'Auvours.

the larger Camp d'Auvours military grounds. Here, between August and December he made over a hundred flights, setting an altitude record of 358ft (109m); culminating on New Year's Eve in a flight of 2 hours, 20 minutes and 23 seconds, which won the Michelin Prize of 20,000 francs (about $4,000). Crowds flocked from throughout Europe to see the acclaimed flights, and Wilbur made sixty ascents with delighted passengers. These included a woman, Madame Hart O. Berg, her skirts tied around her ankles with string!

revolutionized, and its pioneers accepted the truth of the brothers' earlier flights. "Who can now doubt that the Wrights have done all they claimed?" Réne Gasnier asked, "We are as children compared with the Wrights."

Wilbur made a further nine flights in five days at Hunaudières before moving to

Wilbur conquered Europe with his incredible flying, but refused to give public speeches about it. He once remarked: "I know of only one bird, the parrot, that talks, and it can't fly very high."

The death of Lieutenant Selfridge

While Wilbur was making his triumphant first flights in France, Orville transported his Type A airplane to Fort Myer, near Washington D.C. to fly trials for the U.S. Army. He took off for the first time on September 3, 1908, and the *Washington Post* reported: "When the machine finally soared into the air, everyone became afflicted with a mild form of emotional insanity" with "cheers, hand-clapping and altogether undignified prancing . . . It was a magical moment."

Orville made ten flights, including four of over an hour's duration, before fitting longer propellers in a bid to meet the army's 40mph (64kph) speed requirement. On September 17, he took up the modified airplane, with Lieutenant Thomas Selfridge as his passenger. A propeller blade cracked, sheering a rudder wire, and the aircraft plummeted to the ground from about 150ft (46m). Orville was

Wilbur demonstrates the airplane to King Alfonso of Spain.

dragged from the tangle of wood and crumpled cloth, suffering fractures to his hip, leg and ribs. Selfridge, his skull fractured on impact, died a few hours later. He was the first person to be killed in an airplane accident.

This tragedy did not diminish the importance of Orville's flights, and the Wright brothers' achievements were at last recognized in their own country. The army tests were suspended, and after leaving hospital Orville, with his sister Katharine, joined Wilbur in Pau, southwestern France. Wilbur taught three French pilots to fly, before traveling to Italy where he gave instruction to two Italian lieutenants. The brothers were visited by many of Europe's heads of state, before making a triumphant homeward tour, receiving honors in Paris, London and New York. They had introduced the air age to the world.

Orville was seriously injured and his passenger killed, in the crash at Fort Myer.

The flight of the Bishop

The Wright brothers' influence upon aviation was at its peak in 1909. New pioneers followed their example, building improved airplanes, and creating a European air age. In July, aviation's popularity was greatly increased by Louis Blériot's magnificent flight across the English Channel. In August, Reims, in France, hosted thirty-eight airplanes in the world's first great aviation meeting.

After returning to Dayton, where a holiday was declared in their honor, Wilbur and Orville traveled to Fort Myer to complete the army trials. For a month, Orville gracefully circled the parade ground in a new "Signal Corps" machine. He exceeded both speed and endurance requirements, and in August the army purchased the machine for $30,000. Orville then traveled to Germany, where he took Prince Wilhelm into the air, trained two German pilots and established a new Wright Company. Wilbur, meanwhile, was paid a huge fee to fly around the Statue of Liberty, where millions of New

Yorkers were gathered to celebrate the anniversary of the discovery of the Hudson River. In October, he trained the first two American pilots, and took up the United States' first woman passenger.

The Wright Company was formed in November to manufacture the brothers' airplanes and guard their patents in America. A former hot-air balloonist, Roy Knabenshue, was hired to organize exhibitions, while Orville began training pilots to demonstrate the Wright airplanes. In 1910, a flying school was established at Huffman Prairie, where the Wrights even built a flight simulator to train pilots for their display team.

On May 25, 1910, the brothers made their only joint flight ever, with Orville at the controls. Orville later took up their 82-year-old father for his only flight, to the Bishop's excited cries of "Higher, Orville, higher!"

Orville takes his father up on his father's only flight.

The end of the partnership

The Wright brothers' momentous invention founded the age of flight.

Having learned the value of advertising from their days in the bicycle trade, Wilbur and Orville used their display team to demonstrate Wright airplanes at the air-shows that promoted aviation throughout America.

They continued to improve their machines, and by 1910 had developed the Model B. This machine, with a tail rudder instead of a front elevator, and a wheeled undercarriage replacing the traditional skids, more closely resembled a modern airplane. Orville also raced in a specially built "Baby Grand" airplane which attained speeds exceeding 70mph (112kph). In 1911, Orville returned to flying gliders, and established a world duration record.

On May 30, 1912, Wilbur Wright, aged forty-five, died of typhoid fever. His father's diary remembered, "A short life full of consequences. An unfailing intellect, imperturbable temper, great self-reliance and as great modesty, seeing the right clearly, pursuing it steadily, he lived and died." Orville was devastated and became increasingly reclusive in his later years. He continued to fly until 1918, constantly defended the patents protecting his and Wilbur's inventions, and maintained a lifelong involvement in aviation.

The original Flyer airplane was sent to the Science Museum in London in 1928, when the Smithsonian Institution refused to recognize it as the first aeroplane to fly! They later apologized, and the Flyer was returned for exhibition at the Smithsonian, following Orville's death on January 30, 1948.

Through painstaking study and practical experiment, the Wright brothers carefully and brilliantly created the first airplane. Their invention transformed the world, and created a new era in history. On the twenty-fifth anniversary of their first flight, a memorial was unveiled at Kill Devil Hill bearing this quotation from the Greek poet Pindar: "O'er the fruitful earth, athwart the sea hath passed the light of noble deeds unquenchable forever."

Important dates

1867   Wilbur Wright born near Millville, Indiana (April 16).

1871   Orville Wright born in Dayton, Ohio (August 19).

1889   They publish the *West Side News*.

1892   The Wrights start their bicycle business.

1899   They construct and fly a biplane kite.

1900   The Wrights fly in their first glider.

1901   They fly their second glider.

1901–2   The Wrights conduct extensive research into flight.

1902   They fly nearly 1,000 flights in their third glider.

1903   The Wrights make the world's first airplane flight.

1904   The Wrights build and fly Flyer II.

1905   The Wrights build and fly Flyer III.

1905–8   The Wright brothers quit flying temporarily.

1908   The Wrights win contracts in both the United States and also in France. Wilbur flies in France. Orville flies U.S. Army trials at Fort Myer. Lt. Selfridge is killed.

1909   The Wrights fly in Europe. Orville completes U.S. Army trials. Wright Company formed.

1912   Wilbur dies of typhoid fever (May 30).

1948   Orville dies (January 30).

Glossary

Altitude   Height above the ground.
Biplane   Airplane with two sets of wings, one above the other.
Elevator   Surface controlling an airplane's climb and descent.
Flight simulator   Apparatus simulating flight, to train pilots on the ground.
Genesis   Origin or beginning of something.
Glider   An unpowered airplane.
Patent   Acknowledgment of exclusive right to make or sell a new invention.
Penny farthing   Old type of high bicycle, with a large front wheel.
Pusher propeller   A propeller placed behind an airplane's wings and engine.
Warp   To twist an airplane's wings to alter their lift.
Wind tunnel   Apparatus for producing constant airstream to measure effect of wind pressure on different surfaces.

Books to read

Air and Flight by Neil Ardley (Franklin Watts, 1984)
Aircraft by Bill Gunston (Franklin Watts, 1986)
Epic Flights: Trailblazing Air Routes by David Jefferis (Franklin Watts, 1988)
The Story of Flight by Jim Robins (Warwick Press, 1987)

Index